The Waiting Room

The Waiting Room

DOMINIQUE RISPOLI

RESOURCE *Publications* • Eugene, Oregon

THE WAITING ROOM

Copyright © 2021 Dominique Rispoli. All rights reserved. Except for brief quotations in critical publications or reviews, no part of this book may be reproduced in any manner without prior written permission from the publisher. Write: Permissions, Wipf and Stock Publishers, 199 W. 8th Ave., Suite 3, Eugene, OR 97401.

Resource Publications
An Imprint of Wipf and Stock Publishers
199 W. 8th Ave., Suite 3
Eugene, OR 97401

www.wipfandstock.com

PAPERBACK ISBN: 978-1-6667-0712-0
HARDCOVER ISBN: 978-1-6667-0713-7
EBOOK ISBN: 978-1-6667-0714-4

06/24/21

To the one who wants me.

Contents

PROLOGUE

The Waiting Room II	3

PART 1: THE LONGING

Winter Reverie	7
Two Years, Four Days	8
Autumn Blues	9
Concrete Flowers	10
Even As I Soar	11
February Nights	12
A Poet's Problem	13
Prey	14
A Study Of A Memory	15

PART 2: THE FANTASY

Lack Of Eloquence	19
You	20
Known	21
In My Dreams	22
Alexa, Play Almost Lover By A Fine Frenzy	23
Ancient Of Days	24
Candy Hearts	25
Bodies Floating	26

Anchors Away	27
The Waiting Room	28
Afternoon Delight	29
The Opposite Gender	30
Awkward Years Revisited	31
Leftovers	32
An Ode To The Bath	33
Control	34
Bleeding Heart	35

PART 3: THE REBIRTH

I Wrote This While You Were Ignoring Me	39
Vessels	40
Light Bulbs	41
The Same Song	42
Hollow	43
The Office	44
Onwards	46
Rapunzel's Melody	47
Disordered Thinking	48
Creature Of This House	49
The Search	50
I Am, I Am, I Am	52
Ordinary Days	53
An Ode To Florida	54
Fire & Stars	55

EPILOGUE

Waiting Revisited	59

Prologue

THE WAITING ROOM II

I am sitting in this waiting room made up of windows and a door. Though the door only opens from the outside. I am stuck in this waiting room made up solely of windows. Only one person has the key, did I mention that? That person is unaware he has the key. So he walks by, blissfully ignorant that my freedom rests in his hands. I scream and bang on the windows, but he does not hear me. He walks by again, and again, and again, ignoring my pleas, and each time he walks by I lose my resolve little by little. I eventually come to terms with the fact that this is where I will stay. In this waiting room. Wasting away to nothing. Until one day he finally realizes, and opens the door, but by then I am nothing but dust and dead promises.

PART 1

The Longing

WINTER REVERIE

I will always have
a small sort of hope
tucked away
in the dustiest corner of my heart
that one day,
on some wintry afternoon,
you will show up
with love in your eyes
and me the only one on your mind.

TWO YEARS, FOUR DAYS

Abruptly, you reached out, and just as quickly, you turned away. Silent exits are your specialty, and missing you is mine. Two years older and I am still trying to make sense of it all. The way we'd dance around each other and the doors that would slam shut on our unspoken feelings. How I tried to reach out, but you were pulled away by God knows what, and I was left to pick up the pieces. Two years clean, but my heart still aches when I catch a glimpse of your face. And I still count the time by how long it's been since I last saw you. You messaged me four nights ago and my hopes shot up so high they've not come down since. Though, once again we found ourselves dancing around each other and putting up walls draped with polite conversation. I wanted so badly to tear those walls down, but you drifted away before I got the chance. And gentle but firm arms kept me from running after you, leaving me with a mind filled to the brim with things left unsaid and hands grasping for answers to shed light on your sudden and violent change of heart. Did it hurt you to talk to me? Do you believe me to be so disenchanted with you that you figured you could walk away with no disclosure and without a second glance? But, what you can't see is the dull ache that has made its home in my chest ever since I met you, and how it has bloomed and blossomed each time I've had to let go of you. You can't see the way your name is etched into the back of my mind , and how your face frequents my dreams. If only we could get on the same page. But, we are both reaching and always missing. Pulled away by our own misconceptions and each too haunted by the memory of each other. What could have been sings us its relentless tune, but the hushed song of hope is what I strain to listen to.

AUTUMN BLUES

As summer's warm light began to fade, I felt you beginning to reach out. Warmth and light conversation filled the air, I floated on a cloud filled with hope. Then summer began to flicker, and it finally went out. And you disappeared. I wonder how many times you are to vanish before you are here to stay. I wonder how many times I am supposed to let you slip through my fingers before your fingers are permanently in mine.

CONCRETE FLOWERS

I'm trying to resurrect us with my old feelings.
Maybe if I think about the old times enough,
new times will grow between the cracks.
Like plants grasping towards the sky
between slabs of concrete,
I am grasping for you.

EVEN AS I SOAR

You are stuck in my head like a bad song on the radio.
I want to take the radio out of the car
and smash it.
But, that won't get the song out of my head.
Because it's inside of me now.
You are a part of me now.
There is before you and after you
no in between.
You are tucked away in the dusty corners of antique stores.
Memories that are defined by how much I've missed you.
The thought of you so strong it left an imprint on that moment.
Forever tinted by my sharp longing for you.
Some things change.
We grow older
Time moves quicker,
but one thing never changes
and that is how I feel for you.
Oh, I've tried
I've tried to shed you like a snake would shed its skin,
like a butterfly leaves behind her cocoon.
But even as I soar,
I always come back to you.

FEBRUARY NIGHTS

I crave simpler times,
car rides to nowhere in particular,
and you laughing so hard you're silent.
Eerily dark early nights
and the bitter cold prickling my skin.
When responsibilities were light
and the only thing I had to worry about
was us being pushed together.
Now I'm crumbling under the weight of obligation.
Adulthood and anxieties are knocking at my door,
but you're still nowhere to be found.

A POET'S PROBLEM

I'm not sure how many poems I can write about you. I can take you out of your box in my heart and study you. Run my hands over you like you run your hands over an old book. It creeks as you open it, disrupting the spine. Old but treasured. This is how I treat my memories of you. Because that's all there is now, memories. Memories like light from a stained glass glistening across the floor. Beautiful even if only seen in fragments. But soon the sun will go down, and the books will be put back on the shelf. The memories will fade. My only wish is that you remain.

PREY

Like a flash of light in the corner of my eye,
I think I see you but I turn and you are gone.
You are always present but never here.
You are in the faces of strangers
as I walk through the mall.
The cold winter breeze pricking my skin,
taking me back to the nights when I would walk from one building to
the next.
And you tried to coax me into your car,
but I just wouldn't let myself
let myself let go.
I avoided you like a bad habit,
but all you were was smiles dripping with possibility
and I treated you like a predator hunting for its prey.
I was the prey.

A STUDY OF A MEMORY

We spent all day together.
I was glued to your side.
Involuntarily, but glued nonetheless.
Oh, I loved it.
I wanted to be stuck to you always.
Following you wherever you went.
I just loved looking at you.
Talking to you.
The words that flowed out of your mouth like liquid gold to me,
and your eyes like melting chocolate in the sunlight.
Towards the end of that beautiful Sunday
you asked me to go with you outside.
I panicked like I did around you,
and said no.
You almost looked dejected.
This was the littlest of moments,
the tiniest of a memory.
But, I still regret that answer.
What I really wanted to say was yes,
yes, I'll go with you.
I'd follow you off the edge of this cliff.
Right into the ocean.
the unknown.
I'd follow you anywhere.
And I think that's what scared me.
So, I said no.

Years later I still pull out this memory
and weep over it,
because what I would give
to follow you anywhere today.
What I would tell myself
is don't take him for granted,
because someday you are going to ache, and ache, and ache.
Ache to follow him somewhere, anywhere.
But you lost your chance,
he doesn't want you now.

PART 2

The Fantasy

LACK OF ELOQUENCE

I am sorry that I am unable to speak
with the eloquence that can paint pictures and move mountains.
But, instead my words trip over one another or get lost
once they leave my lips.
So, I've chosen to stay silent
because it is easier to bear than fumbled words and mumbled
apologies.

YOU

I cannot imagine
how deep Your love must be.
For even when I stray,
You gently take me by the hand
and lead me back to You.
And when doubt and confusion
are infiltrating my mind,
You whisper to my heart
with a voice as soft as rainfall.
Promises of Peace
and a reminder
that no matter what storm
I find myself in,
You are right there
holding me through the chaos.

KNOWN

What do I know?
I know nothing.
I am known by no one
except One.

IN MY DREAMS

You only visit me in my dreams.
Soft, the outline of you hazy.
Whispers and shadows,
we waltz around each other.
Twirling, you hold me close.
With ornate designs on the walls,
and a sparkling crystal floor.
The scene shifts, and we are in a meadow.
You put a flower behind my ear and grab my hand.
Pulling me close, and planting a kiss on my forehead.
Suddenly, the world melts away and I am awoken.
I am left with only a feeling
an echo of you.
as my memory of us together fades,
I start my day with a murmur of your presence surrounding me,
and holding me.

ALEXA, PLAY ALMOST LOVER BY A FINE FRENZY

I can't look at your face.
It is a reminder of what almost was.
A reminder of the sweet words that flowed from your mouth.
A reminder of the times we spent in your car, driving to nowhere in particular.
Your hand casually patting my leg in intervals
during light conversation.
A reminder of your plans and seemingly eagerness to talk to me.
A reminder of what could have been.
I'm not sure what happened between now and then.
What caused you to drift away, the tide carrying you in. Leaving not even a trace.
Do I miss you? Or do I miss how you made me feel?
You made me feel light and hopeful. Like I finally found it this time.
Like I found the one who would stay.
But you didn't.

ANCIENT OF DAYS

I'm going to be dying.
Ancient of days, on my deathbed
and I'll still be stuck in an avalanche of feelings for you
collapsing over me like a waterfall
throwing me into the rocks below.
I was never told
that loving someone would cause so much pain,
but it's unrequited love
that hurts the most.
It comes over you in waves and never leaves,
leaving you stranded on an island
with only your empty hands to keep you company.

CANDY HEARTS

I am so bitter.
Filled to the brim with it.
Bubbling over and spilling out.
I try to hide it,
hold it all inside.
But, it leaks out in conversations.
Rolling out of my mouth before I can stop it.
Phrases and words
all said in light tones but soaked in vinegar.
Do you even think about me?
Of course you don't.
I will never understand why I am destined to observe,
never experience.
Candy hearts are on the tongues of some,
There is just dirt on mine.

BODIES FLOATING

I am drowning in a sea of nose,
the waves tossing me and slamming me against the shore again
and again.
Indifference surrounds me and drags me down deeper.
Inhaling the salt water,
I try to choke down the denials.
Rejection scraping my lungs,
hollow words and polite hellos
ring in my ears.
As I sink to the bottom.

ANCHORS AWAY

The sinking feeling of an anchor dropping down
to the bottom of the sea,
Hopelessness.
Waves slamming you against the shore again and again
gasping for air and only getting lungs full of sand.
A lifeless body being spit out by the ocean
the tide gently caressing it
like you would caress a sick child
only to pull it back in.
Where it will be swallowed by the depth,
remembered no more.

THE WAITING ROOM

Why are we still here?
Scratching and pulling at your skin,
trying to find the answers in your silent stares and unspoken phrases,
I am tired of wrestling with it so I just push it aside,
hoping to hide the discontent I feel
and the anger bubbling up inside,
too tired to beg for it anymore,
too ignorant to understand.
I am sitting in a waiting room while the clock laughs at me.
Mocking my helpless state.
Hopeless but still waiting.
This is how I will always remain,
even when I am long gone.
My bones scattered in that waiting room
Hopeless but still Waiting

AFTERNOON DELIGHT

In the afternoon is where most of the sadness lies, waiting for me. Despite the sparkling sun reaching across the sky, there it sits, mocking me. It's tucked away in the midday coffees and tireless tasks. Some days it ticks softly like the clock in my office, some days it screams loudly like a toddler waking up from her nap, just when you had a moment of peace and quiet. It disrupts and distorts. The brightness of the day hurts my eyes, it weighs me down until it seems like I just can't get up again. It looks like unwashed hair, and dirty dishes piling in the sink. It's hoods over my head and shaky hands. Everyday the clock strikes one, and I am undone.

THE OPPOSITE GENDER

"I hate men"
I say, the bitter words leaving my tongue,
I recite it over and over again in my head like a mantra,
But I don't really
I hate that every one that I have ever opened my heart to has left me,
returned like a shirt that didn't quite fit right.
Not one has found something in me worth staying for.
I hate the way men have made me feel,
small and not worth knowing,
wanted for a minute and forgotten the next.
All should not have to answer for the carelessness of a few.
But it's hard to separate the two
when all you've known is
stale affection and empty promises,
lies that trickle from lips like honey.
Sweet one minute and rotten the next.
Boys disguised as men,
all plan and no action.
All word and no deed.
What business do you have starting this fire in me
if you're not around
to tend to it?

AWKWARD YEARS REVISITED

I feel fourteen. Awkward and unwanted.

Braces stuck to my teeth and lacking enough knowledge to know when I deserve better. Middle school for me was filled with emotions so deep you could drown in them with no one who wants to swim. Eight years later and this is still my song. I thought by now some things would have changed. But my mind is still racing as fast as he lost interest in me, and I am still clinging to someone who wants nothing to do with me.

LEFTOVERS

I am so weary.

I am surrounded by light, but all I can feel is the darkness creeping into my soul. Burrowing, making its home in me. I am surrounded by laughter, but all I can focus on is the heaviness of my heart.

I wish I could just stick my hand into my chest and pull out the melancholy. I wish I could reason with it. "You have no home here!" I'd cry, throwing it into the sea. It would sink to the bottom and consume me no more.

AN ODE TO THE BATH

The bathtub is draining,
and I refuse to get out of it.
It trickles down slowly but surely all around me,
all suds and tepid water.
But wait.
A washcloth blocks the drain
causing the process to slow.
The faucet drips wildly in disapproval.
The bubbles I put in only moments earlier cling to the sides of the tub
trying to elongate their lifespan.
The water is getting lower now.
I sink to the bottom of the tub
letting myself be pulled into the current
and sucked down the drain.

CONTROL

It's like a stabbing in my gut,
a sharp wave of terror,
the sensation you are not in control,
I'm not in control
I need to be in control.
My mind races and gets lost in itself,
my hands shake and reach out
But no one is there to grasp onto.

BLEEDING HEART

There was nothing poetic about the way you left me. Abruptly and silently, without any warning. I kept coming back though, like a criminal returning to the scene of a crime because they got some sick satisfaction from it. I kept knocking on your door and demanding you notice me. My bleeding heart in my hands, begging you to take it. But your hands were full and you had places to be.

PART 3
The Rebirth

I WROTE THIS WHILE YOU WERE IGNORING ME

Wait, wait, wait
But I'm tired
I'm tired
I'm tired
I'm tired of staring at a screen hoping you'll text
but you don't.
My words flying through the webs of your indifference
and getting lost trying to reach you.
There is still so much I want to say to you,
but you don't want to hear it.
We are now two totally different people
with lives lived separately for far too long.
My skin is not the same skin you've touched.
Your mind is not the same mind I fell in love with.
I keep hanging on to this insufferable hope,
but, I really want to forget you.
I need to forget you
I need to clean you out of my heart's closet,
and make room for someone new.
Oh, it's time.
It's time to let you go.

VESSELS

I wish I could crawl out of my own skin,
shed like a snake would and start anew,
my darkness interwoven
within the rotting flesh now laying on the floor.
But no
The darkness is inside of me,
so take out each organ
one by one,
and then nothing else is left
but the hollowness of my bones
and my aching muscles
until I am nothing but an empty vessel.

LIGHT BULBS

It is so dark in this room.
The only light that remains
is emanating weakly from the small bulbs in the kitchen.
I am sitting in a brightly lit area
looking out into the dark kitchen.
I feel safer in the darkness.
Everything is soft and hides a multitude of sins,
while in the light it's harsher and everything is laid bare.
I'm not sure where I am going with this,
but all I know is I am supposed to be in the light,
but I feel drawn to the darkness.
Maybe it's the darkness inside of me.
My tendency to hide
and the weeds growing inside
recognizing the darkness outside

THE SAME SONG

Contentment is what I seek.
Looking under every rock until I find it.
Contentment is off with Purpose,
nowhere to be found & killing my Peace of mind.
I want to always be in action and know where I am going,
but everything is still and there are several paths all covered in thorns.
People say it will get better but will it?
It seems like life is just a terrible song stuck on repeat,
and the record player is broken
so the only thing there is left to do is to destroy it to stop the noise.

HOLLOW

I am hollow.
Yet I am so full
full of desire
desire to be
desire to grow,
desire to become so much more than I already am,
to do so much more than I already am doing.
I am trapped
in a skin full of anxieties and regrets.
Bubbling up to the surface,
drowning out the good.
My motivation and drive
crushed under the weight of my skin's indifference.
I am trapped in a cage
where I have the key.
But no strength to put it in the lock.

THE OFFICE

I am anxious in the psychiatrist's waiting room.
A place where I should feel safe,
my heart beating against my rib cage like it's trying to escape.
I'm afraid of what she'll say.
That I'm not sick.
That this is just how I am.
These racing thoughts and mood swings that soar higher than a child
on a swing set trying to touch the sky
are just me
and that there is no cure,
no medication or pill to prescribe to my brand of crazy.
I watch the fish in the tank chase each other,
The clock ticks.
I realize most of my life is spent in waiting rooms.
The fish are still now.
I've still not been called.
The suspense made my hands shake.
Business women and people in sweats pass me by,
I wonder what's wrong with them,
what decay is in their brain like mine.
I hate waiting.
It's been 20 minutes
my senses are so heightened
like a dog with its hair rising on its back,
alert and ready to attack.
This is what my disorder does to me.

Like a bird darting it's head around
looking for it's foe.
Never calm
always awake
so awake.

ONWARDS

I am on the cusp of something.
A change of pace.
Flipping my world upside down.
Fear reaches its arms towards me,
but I refuse to fall into them.
Here I stand
in the midst of my fear
ready to face
whatever comes next.

RAPUNZEL'S MELODY

I want to live.
I want to feel the sun on my face
bury my feet in the warm sand
curl my toes and feel alive.
My mind is my prison.
My thoughts are my shackles.
I am stuck in routine
desperate to break free.
I don't know what I want.
I definitely don't know what I need.
I want to feel like I am living
not stuck in my tower.
Watching people from afar
leading lives that I wish I could lead.
I am Rapunzel
wondering when my life will begin
when all along
I have the power.
The power to change my life
To make it how I want it to be
I am stuck,
but I long to be free. . .

DISORDERED THINKING

I am safe
wrapped in the cocoon of routine.
Familiarity surrounds me,
my anxious mind locks me in place
surrounding me in lies.
Comfort zones are safe.
Comfort zones can be permanent.
No. . .
Comfort zones are holes you dig yourself in,
trapping you in the mundane.
You are only truly alive
if you step out of your comfort zone.

CREATURE OF THIS HOUSE

I am a creature of this house
locked inside it's suffocating embrace.
A patient in a bed
Too sick to move
But the sickness is in my head
and it is wrapping me in chains.
The house creaks and sighs
as I sigh along with it.
If these walls could talk
they'd tell of my deepest secrets,
the things I do behind closed doors
that no one knows but me.
This house is my confidant.
And I am it's friend.
It's watched me grow up.
It has watched me leave,
bags packed and piled into a car,
it's seen me come back,
my tail between my legs.
Back to the familiar and safe.
Now here I am
Six months later
Still in this house
I am a creature of this house.

THE SEARCH

Every decision I've ever made has been a wrong one.
Should I stay or should I go?
Either way I won't be satisfied.
My contentment has been dead for some time now.
Is it possible to be in two places at once?
pulled in different directions
taking but never giving
'Contentment is a choice,' she says,
but what if no matter what I choose I never find it?

But contentment is a choice.
It's taking a moment to pause
and notice the little things.
It's laying in the opposite room
while your mother sings and cleans the dishes,
listening to the faucet run
Slow and Steady
It's staring at the ceiling,
contemplating everything you've been through these past six months.
Picking up and moving 2,000 miles away,
All alone.
Crying in the kitchen putting groceries away
and walking around in crowds but feeling utterly lonely.
It's also a stranger calling you brave
when you've never even considered it.

It's deciding enough is enough
and closing a chapter of unknowns
while going back to what is familiar.
Not a failure but a Lesson
An Experience
Is this contentment?
Realizing that no decision is a wrong decision,
but everything happens for a reason.
And everything we go through is not an accident,
but a journey to shape us into who we are meant to be

I AM, I AM, I AM

I am the moon reflecting the sun. Not as bright, but still emanating light. I am all the words left unsaid, neglected by you and long forgotten. I am so much more than what you think. I am the oceans deep, filled to the brim with vibrant life. I am the birds soaring high above on their way to a better place. There are complex ecosystems and constellations inside of me. I am so much more than I appear, hiding it all neatly inside. The only hint is the glimmer in my eye.

ORDINARY DAYS

It's funny how one song
or a whiff of a scent
can bring back so much.
It can wrap its arms around you
and take you to simpler times
like sitting on the floor in the living room
those Sunday afternoons waiting for lunch to be ready,
or friendships that have since faded away
as time trickled by. . .
I take these memories out
and revisit them once and awhile,
running my fingers along the worn edges.

Did we know?
Did we know that these everyday moments
will soon become dreams?
The simplest of occasions becoming treasures almost forgotten.
What we would give to go back
to those seemingly ordinary days.
That is why we must hold close the time we have now.
Because soon they will become distant as well.
And then we would give anything to go back to this present
moment.
Now a memory.

AN ODE TO FLORIDA

I crave the warmth on my skin. The sunshine glistening on the wet concrete, the palm trees swaying in the light breeze. You are hazy in my memory, brightened by my sweet nostalgia. Things weren't as good as I make them out to be, but I still long. I long for the orange hinted smells, and the painted sunsets. I am where I'm supposed to be now. The familiar traded for the new. But I still wonder. Wonder if we will ever meet again.

FIRE & STARS

I have fire and stars in my veins.
oceans in my mind
sparkling and shimmering
reflecting the morning sun.
Inside of me are whole worlds
but it takes time
for me to reveal this side.
Pull me back
Layer by Layer
and soon you will see
the light sparkling through the cracks
the water streaming out to caress your feet.
Please be patient with me
I am worth the effort.
The raveling and unraveling of my soul
is a process
and if you stay long enough,
you will see.

Epilogue

WAITING REVISITED

"Will you wait for me?"
Muttered so softly I almost couldn't hear you. Time slows, and I can see your hand reaching towards me. Your eyes, soft and dripping with love. I don't know what I did to deserve this. My mind goes back to all the nights I ignored you, seething with anger at the matches you wouldn't let me play with. All the times I forgot you and ran away with my selfish desires. Why is it you want me again? My lack of understanding turns to self doubt, and I run away. Back to the poison that lives inside of me. I just want you. All I've ever wanted is you. Why do I keep staring at a reflection when I can have the whole sunset?

Thank you so much for reading!
If you want updates on the author and more,
connect with her here!

Website: Http://DominiqueRispoliWrites.com
Instagram: @DominiqueRispoliWrites

www.ingramcontent.com/pod-product-compliance
Lightning Source LLC
Chambersburg PA
CBHW060426050426
42449CB00009B/2164